Return Unto Me
by Megan Ulrich

Eternal rest grant to them, O Lord;
and let perpetual light shine upon them.
May their souls,
and the souls of all the faithful departed,
through the mercy of God,
rest in peace.

Amen

Copyright © 2020 by Megan Ulrich
Illustrations © 2020 by Katie Grugin

Edited by Stephen Johnson

All rights reserved. No part of this book may be reproduced or used in any manner without written permission of the copyright owner except for the use of quotations in a book review. For more information, visit http://www.megan-ulrich.com/.

FIRST EDITION
ISBN: 9780578732800
LCCN: 2020921401

Dedication

For those parents who will never again hold their children on this side of Heaven.

For the blessing of my children.

For my sweet, sweet husband and his love for our family.

And for the Lord of Hosts.

    Thank You.

Please, tread lightly.
The place you are about to enter is holy ground.

Contents

Foreword	9
Litany of Saints	13
17	15
Weston	17
Bailey Marie	19
12.16.19	21
The Big Room	23
4 East	25
Would You Listen if I Told You	27
And the Swallow	29
Homesick	31
Adoration	33
If I Wrote Love Poems,	35
Columbarium	37
Welcome	39
4 Weeks	41
Endnote	43
Discussion Questions	47

Foreword

The three of us got to know Megan when a copy of her book *Hell, Bring the Kids Too* arrived in the mail at one of our parishes with the inscription, "Much love to the dogs", a reference to our podcast "Three Dogs North". It was taken into the confessional that same day for perusal and, it being a slow day for sin, was read in its entirety.

The poems were too good not to share, and pretty soon we all had our own copies of the book. We returned to them often in conversations about grief and love. There was something in them that made us feel more human, and made us want to be more human.

It is a harsh reality that what we truly want is something that we cannot produce ourselves, no matter how hard we try or how many places we look. It is an act of courage to search for life's deepest meaning in the hardest and most mundane places, precisely those places where emptiness and loss are felt most acutely, but that is what those poems did. In *Hell, Bring the Kids too*, we peered into the heart of a mother, wounded and flawed, completely inadequate to the task, yet brimming with the most powerful love that is.

In this collection, too, we see the same fear and sorrow, and the same courage and grace. We see that we are broken, and that life is full of suffering, but we are still worth loving, and life is still worth living. Although the theme of this book is death, the poems do not discourage or depress. Perhaps the reason is that the pain is *dwelt in*. They are not the moody broodings of a teenager, they are a glimpse into the heart of a woman who is trying to let go, to surrender to a love she doesn't understand but that she knows exists because she has loved that way herself. They are an exploration of a broken heart, which somehow contains the consolation of God.

Five stars. Would recommend.

The Dogs are Fr. Connor Danstrom, Fr. Rob Johnson, and Fr. Michael Metz.

Litany of Saints

Levi	Pray for us
Weston	Pray for us
Palmer	Pray for us
Bailey Marie	Pray for us
Michael Thomas	Pray for us
Sawyer Thomas	Pray for us
The Baby They Airlifted to Vandy	Pray for us
The Son of the Man Who Cried at Christmas	Pray for us
and His Little Brother	Pray for us
Those We Could Not Name	Pray for us
All You Mighty Saints	Pray for us

17

My son spent the first 74 days
of his life in a hospital room.
He was a mix of wires then.

They all are, those little 2 lb
pipsqueeks. The 27 weekers.
The ones who are viable.

One day they moved his bed
over a foot or two and I
almost went to someone else's
mix of wires. Because how can you tell,
really, what someone looks like
when you've never seen their face;
When your connection is
based on proximity to the OR
and the familiar blue of the Bili light;
When you don't know what your son smells like
or the color of his eyes.

So maybe I did.
Maybe we brought
home bed 16 instead of 17.

Only we didn't.
We brought home 17.
Our happy lion.
And all the trauma his little body
carried. We brought it all.

And yet,
I still feel

numb.
Like my child's body is here,
but he's already dead.
Like we're all just biding our time until it's over.

Weston

I met your mom on the elevator from 3 East.
We both walked out the
same double doors,
carrying emptied coolers,
reminiscent of
breasts hooked to pumps,
releasing milk to the rhythmic pulse
of a motor.

And I wanted to find solace in her,
in a mutual ache no one else could
understand, because grief shared is
grief lessened and all that bullshit.

Do you have any other kids?

His twin brother.
He died shortly after birth.

It's been two years and
I still say your name.
It's comforting to know that
someone does.

I guess I just thought,
it might as well
be me.

Bailey Marie

I'm not sure I ever got a good glimpse of you.

I saw the vents and the tubes,
but I never really saw
you.

I guess few really did.

The neonatologists and a handful of nurses.
Your mom?
Did she ever see you
without the trimmings and trappings
of grief?
Or did they whisk you away from her,
just a pile of blankets and probes.

Did she stay away because it hurt too much?
      Or not enough?
Or maybe some combination of the two
that's more familiar than
I want to admit.

Did you ever feel her love for you?
Or love at all?
Between the rotation of nurses and volunteers,
did they whisper lullabies in your ear
and hold you on their skin
as their own?

12.16.19

I'm sorry about the title.
No one took the time
to name you,
but that's not really my place.

And I'm sorry that I didn't stop her.
Maybe no one could,
but still,

I would've liked to meet you.

I know she's your mom,
but I can't bring myself to look at her
without anger welling up, spilling
out of my eyes.
And I can't seem to find love for her
or a way to make sense of the
world in light of an earnest
prayer for the oppressed
that went unanswered.

I don't want to see her
the same way
I see you,
as a beloved daughter,
trapped,
scared.

Right now the distance is easier to sit with
and it's safer if
I can't see her in
myself.

In the fear.
In the chaos masquerading as
control.

In the firmly held lie that
no one is coming for me.

The Big Room

The last time I saw you
was in the Big Room.
With your cooler and your purse,
making the slow walk to your isolette.

You used to smile at me
and I to you
as I silently rocked
my son
naked
on my chest.
Methodically going over the
beads in my mind.
Now and at the hour of our death.

I don't know your name
or the child you brought milk to
every day.

But I saw your face in my
agony and you became a part
of that time, to me,
as much as the smell of bleach

and the sound of
automatic locking doors.

It's been 18 months now
and it took me a moment to realize
why I recognized you,
walking out of pediatric rehab
with your son
toddling beside.
Or why I suddenly felt like the
ground was swaying,
a land-locked motion sickness,
like I couldn't grasp my son in front of me,
a spinning I haven't felt in months,
some misplaced nostalgia.

And I wanted to reach out and
hug you.
Tell you we made it.
They're here.

Maybe I'm not the only one who needs to be
convinced.

4 East

The last child I held
was dead for at least twelve hours.
Sometimes life has a way of coming to the end
before it's even started.

The hall was quiet with the deafness of
mourning, but there was a peace in your room
I never want to understand.
And your sweet husband was holding your boy
on his skin like a prayer
and I thought
Oh, to be loved like that.

I did my best to memorize him,
take in the slight fingers and the
soft brown hair,
but I didn't see the color of his eyes
or the tiny little hairs on his tiny little legs.
I never got a chance to hear him say mama
or watch as he
lifted his head for her voice,
but I did hold his body at the same
precise moment as
God.

I still hate when people say things like
He would've started kindergarten this fall
but he would've turned one this winter
and two the next, which feels like
a mounting hurdle as opposed to
the healing of time.

And this whole thing is preposterous
because he's not my son
and there's no way I could understand.
I guess I just wanted to tell you

I miss his slight fingers and
soft brown hair
and I also mourn
for the things we will never know.

Would You Listen if I Told You

It's not your fault.

That sometimes,
most of the time,
there isn't a good explanation.

Would you understand if I told you
there are prayers, and
songs, and well intentioned
comforters, but more than that,
there is pain.

Because it's a lie to hide that from you.

Would you hear me if I told you
that it shouldn't have happened,
not because you failed,
but because suffering is inherent to
living. At least for some of us.

Would you believe me if I told you,
I see you.
Even the parts you are too scared to show
yourself.
And that I still love you even more
because of it.

Would you look me in the eyes
if I told you
You are a good mom.
Not in spite of that day,
but because of the way you have lived since.

And the Swallow

*"Even the sparrow has found a home,
and the swallow a nest for herself,
where she may lay her young."*
   Psalm 84:3

A lifetime ago you told me,
*I don't know what this
means but*

I want to protect you.

But you can't.
One day I will break.
   We all break in time.

But now I hide our
son in my arms
and I can't help it.

I'm sorry.
I didn't realize that
you already knew

the nature of love is loss.

Homesick

I guess, sometimes, there
isn't really much to say.
Just the quiet of longing
and the restlessness that
accompanies it.

And I don't really even know
what I'm after, but I know
there was a time when I found it in your arms.

I can't seem to get lost that easily
anymore.

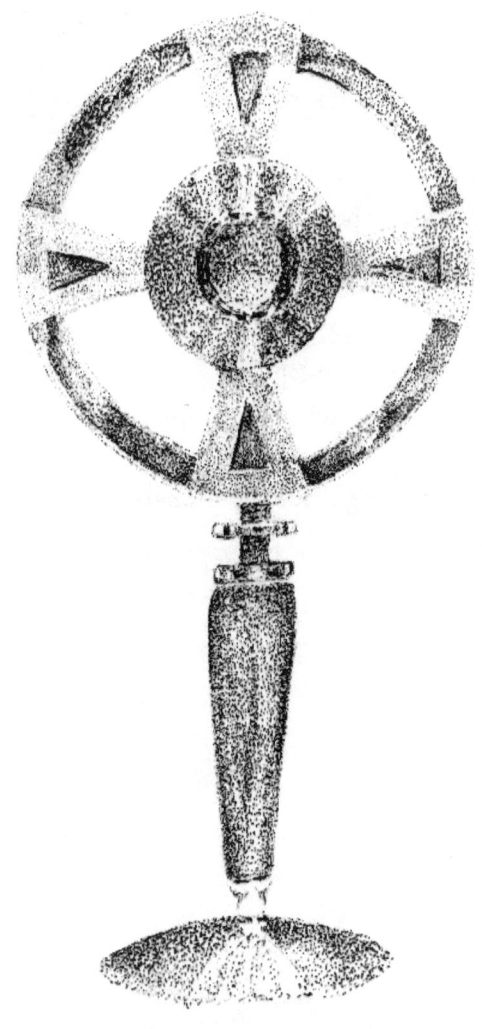

Adoration

There is a quiet here
in this place
that grounds me
to the soil
and the people
and the moments
I am constantly chasing.

And yet,
I never come
      /enough
because sometimes the noise is
too easy.

But there is a quiet here
in this place,
if I let it become
      /a part of
me, it might be
enough.

If I Wrote Love Poems,

I would write one now
about the ache in my heart
when you leave
and this feeling of belonging that
rests somewhere in your chest,
no matter how many times I
wrestle you for it.

So I rest here too,
as I feel the weight of myself
bearing down on you
and I wonder
how much of me can you take?

Columbarium

A friend of mine
never held her son
breathing.

His ashes lay
in a garden near Sacred Heart that
always seems too beautiful a place to bury
hope.

Sometimes, if I'm driving by,
I'll sit with him, for a minute or two,
and we chat, me and my friend's dead son.

And I've never told her this,
but I've often thought,
of the children I'll have someday,
the ones I'll never hold
breathing.

Because this is as beautiful a place as any
to visit, and maybe
if I have a minute or two,
to stay awhile.

Welcome

When your heart lives outside your body.
When you finally have something worth losing.
When the days are filled with joy and fear.
I will stand with you.
I will bear witness.
Because there is something here worth cherishing.

> *Oh Annie girl,*
> *don't you know,*
> *we count the days by you.*

4 Weeks

We're sitting here
at the beginning of everything
just you and I.

And nothing ostensibly
has changed but
everything.

Sometimes I wonder
if Mary had dreams
for her son
like I have dreams for you
that didn't involve kneeling
at the foot of His cross.

Endnote

In many ways, I wrote these poems as a way to heal from my own grief. A grief that no one else seemed to even know existed. After fighting for my son's life for almost 100 days, we brought him home, mostly untouched by his prematurity, and we, my husband and I, found ourselves back to "normal" life, as if there ever could be such a thing. And it seemed at this time, by the healing grace of God, I heard more and more stories of dear friends who were also experiencing the horror of loss, the loss of their children. And I found so much in common with these women, even though my child came home and their children never would. So I did what I always do when I can't articulate my feelings, I wrote about them. What began to emerge was a collection of my own healing. Healing from a loss I never truly experienced, healing from the anxiety that I one day would truly lose everything I had ever loved. And of course the realization that life will continue. That there will be a next day. Whether it's a day I'm prepared for is still unclear to me, but I'm beginning to submit to the providence of God, even though at times I find myself with rather white knuckles.

Discussion Questions

It is my hope that these poems bring healing, especially to those parents who have experienced the death of a child, but healing cannot happen alone; it happens within the support of a loving community. This book and these discussion questions aim to be a launching point for that community.

Before you begin, I recommend laying out some basic small group rules. Above all, remember to love.

1. What are your initial thoughts after finishing the collection?

2. If you are a parent, what poems resonated with your own experience? If you don't consider yourself a parent, what poems surprised you in their relevance to your own life?

3. Many of the poems in *Return Unto Me* explore the idea of accompanying people through grief. In what concrete ways can we better support each other through these times, especially when it feels uncomfortable?

4. If you have experienced the loss of a child, through death, adoption, or physical proximity, what was the best way you were loved by your community? If you felt isolated, how can we better support you in the future?

5. In what concrete ways can we be more courageous in honoring the lives of our children who have died?

6. I wrote "Would You Listen if I Told You" about a specific mom, but in many ways I also wrote it for myself. Is there a woman in your life who needs to hear this from you today? Is it possible that woman is you?

About the Author

Megan Ulrich lives with her husband and two sons in a charming little town in East Tennessee. You can find discussion questions for *Return Unto Me* and additional information about her previous works, including *Hell, Bring the Kids Too*, on her website:
www.Megan-Ulrich.com.

About the Illustrator

Katie Grugin is a Tennessee-born artist and retired Army Officer. A mostly self-taught artist, she uses black and white ink drawings in an attempt to understand the beauty of tiny details in the natural world. She currently lives in Tennessee with her two boxers.

www.ingramcontent.com/pod-product-compliance
Lightning Source LLC
Chambersburg PA
CBHW022000290426
44108CB00012B/1151